Sword of Vengeance

play

Olatubosun David

Mwanaka Media and Publishing Pvt Ltd,
Chitungwiza Zimbabwe

*

Creativity, Wisdom and Beauty

Publisher: *Mmap*

Mwanaka Media and Publishing Pvt Ltd

24 Svosve Road, Zengeza 1

Chitungwiza Zimbabwe

mwanaka@yahoo.com

mwanaka13@gmail.com

https://www.mmapublishing.org

www.africanbookscollective.com/publishers/mwanaka-media-and-publishing

https://facebook.com/MwanakaMediaAndPublishing/

Distributed in and outside N. America by African Books Collective

orders@africanbookscollective.com

www.africanbookscollective.com

ISBN: 978-1-77924-322-5

EAN: 9781779243225

DISCLAIMER

All views expressed in this publication are those of the author and do not necessarily reflect the views of *Mmap*.

PROLOGUE

At a time when power rides on man
As a man on an arrogant horse
The best of friends embraced
Hostility and death

These friends have known peace
And grown in love
In the days of their progenitors
Until a certain time
When power began to ride on man
As a man on an arrogant horse
That the two friendly villages
Embraced hostility and death.

ACT 1
SCENE 1

BALOGUN and his two sons are working in the farm (at the boundary of Alede-Ife and Olofa-Ija Villages)

3

when suddenly they hear a gunshot... his first son is shot by an enemy from Olofa-Ija village.

AKINLABI	Father, the crops are very good this year, don't you notice?
BALOGUN	It is true my son, thanks to the gods
ESAN	But that has always been the experience every year
AKINLABI	Yes, but that of this year is much better as you can see.
ESAN	*Egbon*, you are not wrong. Thanks to the gods of fertility

BALOGUN notices a rodent standing on two legs at a short distance then he quickly calls his sons to stop working and asks them to come over to him.

BALOGUN	AKINLABI! ESAN! Stop the work and come over here quickly.

His sons run to him

AKINLABI	Father, hope there is no problem?
BALOGUN	I sense danger.
AKINLABI	Danger!
BALOGUN	(*Pointing at the rodent*) Look at that front, can you see that?

| | It is a bad omen when you see a rodent in the day light like this. Let us go home. |
| ESAN | What does it symbolize, father? |

A gunshot is heard

| AKINLABI | Yeeeh! Oro oooo! *(He falls, bleeding through the chest and mouth. He dies)* |
| BALOGUN | Ah! *Ta n yin 'bon*? Who shot the gun? |

He rushes and carries him places his head on his laps while he sits on the ground, chanting incantation

AKINLABI o! AKINLABI ooooo!
Akere-so-kebe loruko t' a npe iku
Aro wara-wara bi ojo
L'oruko iwo Alumotu
I've made a covenant of peace with
you concerning my sons
You said whoever knows your name
Shall know no death
You said whoever knows your name
Shall live long
AKINLABI knows your names today
Let his life therefore, be granted unto
him

| ESAN | *(With confidence) Ase waa!* So be it! |

*BALOGUN notices that AKINLABI has given up the ghost, he quickly checks maybe AKINLABI used the **gbekude,** a charm that protects one against sudden death which he prepared for him.*

BALOGUN	Ah! ESAN, your brother didn't use the *gbekude* that I gave him.
ESAN	*(Losing courage)* He must have forgotten to use it. Father can't you still do something? Father plea - - se!
BALOGUN	Ah! *Epa o b' oro mo. Igi da, eye ti fo!* The bird has flown! ESAN, did you make use of your own?
ESAN	Father, I'm always with it all the time. Father, my brother mustn't die like this! *Egbon mi o ma gbodo ku bayii!*
BALOGUN	Ah! *Eni pa gun-nu-gun kii kadun ooo* *Eni p' akalamagbo kii ka 'su* *Eni pa Akinsola t' emi o ni kije.* He who murders a vulture does not live for a year He that murders a vulture does not live for a month Whoever killed my son, Akinsola would not live for seven days

He bears the corps on his shoulder, looks at ESAN courageously.

Omo, ile ya. Home we go.

Curtains close

Scene 2

The bad news is everywhere in the whole village of Alede-Ife. The host of angry army are singing song of war at the front of the king's palace, waiting for the king's blessing to go and fight against Olofa-Ija villge. It is the noise of their song that brings KABIYESI and his CHIEFS out of the palace to speak to them.

LEADER	(*Speaking with anger*) Whoever looks for trouble shall find it!
	Whoever looks for war shall find it!
	Olofa-Ija village has made a fire of war
	It is a must that they are burnt with it
WARRIORS	Ye - - - es!
LEADER	Gidigbo – gidigbo!
WARRIORS	E - - eh!
LEADER	Gidigbo – gidigbo!
WARRIORS	E - - eh!
	Ayunlo ayun bo
	L' owo ny' enu!

7

Ayunlo ayun bo
L' owo ny' enu!

KABIYESI and his CHIEFS come out

KABIYESI   *(Raises his two hands, gesturing to them to stop and listen, then, the noise subsides)*
WARRIORS of our land
Youths of our dear land
I greet you all
I commend your patriotism
I commend your love for Akinyemi
who is no more
In your midst.
The gods of our land will help us avert the death of the youth in this village.
The gods will grant you all long life
And bless you with numerous children

WARRIORS   Ase - - - e!

KABIYESI   We felt what you feel and I pray
Our gods will help us to avert such
an evil occurrence in our land

WARRIORS   Ase - - - e!

KABIYESI   But this is not the right time for us to fight

The eyes of the WARRIORS fall in disappointment. They murmur. But their LEADER speaks.

8

LEADER	KABIYESI
	May you live longer than your
	ancestors.
	KABIYESI, eni ja 'le agbon, agbon a
	ta a
	Eni ja 'we opoto a ri 'ja orun
	Eni ja 'we s' enu a ri 'ja odi
	Olofa-Ija village has made a fire of
	war
	KABIYESI! It is a must
	That they are burnt with it (*he turns to*
	the WARRIORS)
	Abi ki le ni mo wi?
WARRIORS	*(Shout)* You are ri - - - ght!

*Again KABIYESI gestures to them to stop and listen. Then he notices
that one of them is holding a sword, he warns them of its consequence.*

KABIYESI	ESAN, what is that in your hand?
ESAN	(*From the midst of the crowd*) It is the
	Sword of Vengeance, your Highness.
KABIYESI	That sword is too powerful!
	The world it can destroy within a
	moment
	Cannot be rebuilt in a decade.
	So my son, sheathe it. Sheathe your
	sword. Let's embrace peace
ESAN	These enemies have caused a lot of
	disaster in this land.

9

	KABIYESI, shall we continue to look until they completely destroy us? Please KABIYESI, allow us to go and wipe them out at once. Their excesses are getting out of hand.
KABIYESI	But you can't go at this time. And besides, the sword is too powerful.
LEADER	*(His eyes turn red in pain)* KABIYESI, when are we going to fight back or use this sword, if not now?

KABIYESI gestures to one of the CHIEFS to continue the talk.

BOBAJOKO

Eyin odo ilu
Eyin omo ogun
I greet you once again
It's only a bastard who will see a
cause for anger and won't go angry.
You are not bastards
It is also a bastard that would be
entreated and won't listen.

Like KABIYESI has earlier said,
please be calm.
You've always been good
And you've never disappointed us for
once
But listen,

As you've known our tradition
It's a taboo for us to go into war
When we are in a festive mood
Aganyin Festival is just some days
ahead
These people must have definitely
known this;
They want to drag us to war
At a period that our tradition forbids
At a time when our ancestors are
celebrating
When the gods are rejoicing

We won't fight now, so that we don't
incur
The wrath of the gods.
And most importantly,
This is an ancestral sword, we don't
use it anyhow *(He faces the other*
CHIEFS)
Abi ki le ni mo wi?

LADEPO   Baba Oloye, you are right
We are peaceful people
We are not cowards
So let us wait for another time. There
is always another time. *(He gestures to*
KABIYESI to dismiss them)

KABIYESI   You've heard it all
Go home and be peaceful

	Eledua will grant you the courage to bear the loss.
LEADER	KABIYESI, may you live long. We've heard you *(he turns to the WARRIORS)* Gidigbo – gidigbo!
WARRIORS	E - - eh!
LEADER	Gidigbo – gidigbo!
WARRIORS	E - - - eh!
LEADER	My people, we must now return home
	But Olofa-Ija village will surely be made to regret the action of her subjects.
	Fire come, fire go, we must avenge our cause.

They turn and leave. KABIYESI and the CHIEFS enter the palace.

Curtains close

Act 2
Scene 1

OLUBUNMI is coming from the stream. Her mother, who is making fufu at the backyard helps, put down the

water from her head and drinks from it. She pours the
rest inside 'amu': a big pot of clay at their backyard. It
seems the water tastes better and she confesses it.

ASAKE	This water tastes good these days
OLUBUNMI	I noticed it. That was why I stopped fetching from Omi-Ebora.
ASAKE	(*Looks worried*) Then where did you fetch it from?
OLUBUNMI	Mother, you look worried. Why?
ASAKE	I say where did you fetch this water?
OLUBUNMI	(*Pointing a finger*) That place
ASAKE	Which Place?
OLUBUNMI	I fetched from Omi-Ayiye
ASAKE	Ah! Abomination! *Omo yii koba mi po - -o!* This girl has implicated me!

*She turns the whole large quantity of raw fufu she's making away and
breaks the pot of water.*

	We are doomed. We will die before seven days! The villagers mustn't know about this.
OLUBUNMI	(*Looks worried*) Mother, what is wrong?
ASAKE	(*Crying*) Everything is wrong! It is an abomination. Nobody fetches water from that stream. Ah! We are done for! We will die before seven days.

OLUBUNMI	How? You even confessed it just now that the water tasted good. Isn't it better than the Omi-Ebora that smells? Since almost two weeks now that we've been drinking this water, you have been saying the water is good. So why your sudden change of interest now?
ASAKE	Didn't you hear me? I said whoever drinks the water will die before seven days.
OLUBUNMI	Mother, who told you? We've been drinking this water for more than ten days and we have not died.
ASAKE	We've been drinking it for more than ten days! Ten whole days! Ah, and you didn't let me know! We will die before seven days. The water is evil!
OLUBUNMI	No! The villager confessed that our fufu smells nice and tastes good now. So how is the water evil? Tell me mother. You've been saying, for more than a week, that the water is good.
ASAKE	Did I ever say such thing?
OLUBUNMI	Yes, you did.
ASAKE	I thought the gods have purified the Omi-Ebora that we normally fetch; I never knew you've been giving the whole village an abomination.

14

	Anybody that drinks Omi-Ayiye will die before seven days.
OLUBUNMI	You never told me this before and besides, how many people will die before seven days?
ASAKE	Are you, this rat, asking me such a question? Our fathers forbid the village from drinking it and you know that nobody drinks or fetches the water, yet you went to fetch it.
OLUBUNMI	Mother, don't be angry with me. I'm sorry. But why did the ELDERS say nobody should fetch it?
ASAKE	*(Sobbing)* It's a long story
OLUBUNMI	Please don't cry again, tell me the story
ASAKE	Wait till after seven days.
OLUBUNMI	Tell me now
ASAKE	I can't, until after seven days.
OLUBUNMI	Everything is seven days. Will KABIYESI and BALOGUN die before seven days too? Because they've been . . .
ASAKE	*(Cuts in)* Shut up! *Onisokuso.* Nobody must hear it from you that you fetch water from the stream. You heard me?
OLUBUNMI	Yes mother, but we . . .
ASAKE	*(Cuts in)* Shut up and go inside now. (Crying) the ELDERS said, whoever

uses the water for anything will not
live for seven days.

She sobs and sobs, she enters

Curtains close

Scene 2

**Within four days, more than twenty people suddenly
drop dead in the village, leaving almost half of the
villagers in a serious illness. Among the people that
died are KABIYESI and two of his CHIEFS-
BALOGUN and FAFORE- the Ifa priest. This time,
the whole village is calm in despair. People stand in
groups, discussing their woe. Alede-Ife - Village
children including OLUBUNMI, also notice the mood
of their parents, as they speak quietly with one another.**

OLUBUNMI	*(Quietly)* My mother said that whoever fetches or drinks from Omi-Ayiye will die before seven days. I asked her if KABIYESI too will die.
ADUKE	What did your mother say?
OLUBUNMI	She said she didn't know
SULIA	Does that mean KABIYESI has gone to the stream and drink the water?

16

ASAKE overhears OLUBUNMI among her peers, she calls and drags her away from their midst.

ASAKE   OLUBUNMI, what are you doing there? Come over here, you should be hungry by now. (*She drags her away*). Don't implicate me, naughty girl.

OLUBUNMI promises her friends that she will come and continue the story when next they meet again.

OLUBUNMI   I will come and tell you the remaining part of the story after three days.

ASAKE   Shut up! You won't tell them any story.

ASAKE drags OLUBUNMI away. Among other people standing is TALABI and her friend JULI; they are of about forty years each, they are also discussing the issue.

TALABI   It was twenty years ago that something like this happened.

JULI   It is true and that time, it was because the gods were angry. I remember, Ifa Priest said Aganyin, the god of war was angry because we made war against Olofa-Ija villge during Aganyin festive period.

17

TALABI	Aren't we all doomed now that FAFORE the priest and KABIYESI are dead?
JULI	Our elders must do something about it. FAGBEMI the second man to Ifa Priest is as good as FAFORE himself, so we still have hope.
TALABI	They better do something quickly before the villagers leave the village for them. Who knows who is next?
JULI	LADEPO my husband is one of the ELDERS sent to Ilu-Moye village to consult an Ifa Priest over there. Besides, other ELDERS have held a meeting with FAGBEMI.
TALABI	SWhat was the outcome of their meeting?
JULI	I don't know. Maybe they said they need to appease the gods again, but this time not with material things.
TALABI	*(Confused)* Not with material things! With what then?
JULI	*Ore*, I don't know o. You won't hear that from my mouth. I will see you next time. *(She leaves)*
TALABI	*(Soliloquizing)* If not with a goat or dog or cow, what then? Liar. Everyone knows you to be mendacious in this village.

She hisses and as she turns to leave, she starts to hear the sound of a metal gong at a distance, immediately; everyone starts to run for his/her dear life. This sound is odd, it is only used to usher in or announce the procession of a dreaded masquerade in a situation as this. Fear grips her heart, she looks around, everyone is gone. She listens again to discern the direction from which the sound is coming from to know where to run to, then, she starts to hear the voice of TOWN CRIER, shouting at the top of his vice.

TOWN CRIER   Attention! Attention!
Let everyone be attentive.

The gods are angry, the land is vexed
A great woe has trounced the land
And our spirit mothers are silent

For this reason, the ELDERS said
Let everyone, great and small
Citizens and sojourners
Old and young
Male and female
Converge   at   the   village-square
immediately
For a solemn village prayer.
Didn't I speak well?
I spoke well

By this time, men and some women who are bold to come out again respond immediately –

VILLAGERS	You spoke well.

Curtains close

Act 3
Scene 1

At Olofa-Ija Village

The ELDERS and KABIYESI are holding meeting due to their poor harvest. The only option they have is to go and buy food in Alede-Ife - Village.

KABIYESI	*(Clears his throat)* I greet you our ELDERS.
ELDERS	Greetings to you our king. K' oba o pe
KABIYESI	Thank you. I call this meeting so that you elders of our land may help us do something about our poor harvest. We know it has been our usual experience anyway, but the situation is worst this year. It is our adage that says *"agba kii wa l' oja k' ori omo tuntun o wo"*. Yes, responsible ELDERS cannot remain in our land and have their arms folded while they see things go in the wrong. Or what is your opinion?

20

DOPEMU   I greet my king. I greet my fellow ELDERS. This issue of hunger in our land is getting out of hand. We all know that our land is not good for farming, Yet our experience this year is the worst. Isn't the same rain that falls on every land that falls on ours too? We must do something.

OTUN   *(With anger) Hawu!* Who is a stranger in this place or who is a baby? Don't we all know this already? KABIYESI said what is the solution and we expect you to say something. Who doesn't know that we all fart through the anus? Let somebody suggest a solution. That is why we are here.

ADIO   DOPEMU hasn't gone out of the way, abi.

There is a brief silence after which DOPEMU speaks again.

DOPEMU   I suggest we go to Alede-Ife village to buy food.

OTUN   *(With anger)* Abomination!
Hawu! We are not supposed to hear this from your mouth.
Which hunger, tell me, which hunger will ever make a goat eat human faeces? Can it ever be possible? Tell me.

21

ADIO   KABIYESI, our ELDERS, this is a knotty issue but we have the solution right here with us.

The ELDERS adjust themselves with eagerness to hear what he has to say. He proceeds-

Our wives and children are hungry, aren't they? And we all know that Ugbo - Ero, where we normally buy supplement is about one week journey from here and besides, they are taking advantage of our tragedy to make themselves fat and that is why they are selling their goods at extortionate price for us. Therefore, the best and only alternative remains Alede-Ife village. There we can buy food at a cheaper price like my friend, has earlier said. Is anything hard in this matter? No! Let us send our women and let them disguise, like people from a faraway land to Alede-Ife; we will also send some ESCORTS with them. After all, Alede-Ife village is just some hours walk from here and their goods are very cheap or what is difficult in this matter?

22

OLUKOSI	KABIYESI, how can we stoop so low to the extent of going in search of food to the land of the beasts? It will be too ridiculous. KABIYESI, I suggest we rather die in hunger than do such a silly thing.
KABIYESI	*(Clears throat)* ELDERS of our land, I thank you all. I too will not support going to Alede-Ife village just because we want to eat. Let us mask our tears with a smile. We are honourable people. But since there is no solution in the sight, please go now and come back with alternative solution in three days' time.

KABIYESI enters, the ELDERS dismiss

Curtains close

Act 4
Scene 4

Alede-Ife Village

Some officials of the government agency for health care delivery arrive Alede-Ife village to give free health services to the people due to the mass death they are experiencing and to find out the cause. They call the people together and address them.

SPOKESPERSON   Our elders, we greet you.

We greet our mothers and everybody.

We heard about your tragedy and we are here to sympathise with you.

May God help us avert evil in this village.

PEOPLE   Ase - - -e

SPOKESPERSON   Our people, your joy brings happiness to our heart

And your health is our wealth.

However when you are sad, every other village and city is sad.

Therefore, please accept our heartfelt condolence.

PEOPLE   Thank you.

SPOKESPERSON   We are here to give you free health services. That is, we will test you, treat you and give you drugs free of charge. So it is very important that you all come out when we call for you. This is how we will do it. We will first attend to your little children

	before we attend to the adults and as you can see, the time is already gone today; the treatment will have to start tomorrow.
BOBAJOKO	Our people from the city we thank you all. May the gods of our land bless you. *(He clears throat)*
	Please we truly need your help to put an end to this trouble.
	Like you said, we will come out.
	Sebi ke saa ti fun wa l' abere, ka tun gb' oogun naa lo ba tan.
	We will come. *(He faces the crowd)* you have heard what they said. Tomorrow, nobody should go to farm ...
A WOMAN	*(Cuts in) Se oro oko ree to wa nle yii. Be tie ni a ma jeun, a ti setan.*
	If at all you say we shouldn't eat, we are ready.
BOBAJOKO	Rara o. nobody said you shouldn't eat. Please wake up quickly tomorrow and cook for your children, let them come out by the first cockcrow in the morning.
SPOKESPERSON	No sir. That will be too early. The treatment will start by nine o'clock in the morning.
BOBAJOKO	*(To the SPOKESPERSON)* E seun dokita wa.

25

	(*Back to the crowd*) Can you hear that?
PEOPLE	*Bee ni*. We've heard him.
BOBAJOKO	That is good. You may now go back to your houses.

The VILLAGERS leave, the ELDERS walk to the medical personnel to thank and shake hands with them.

Curtains close

Scene 2

The CHIEFS invite FAGBEMI to council's meeting in order to know what Ifa has to say about what is happening in the village. Every one of the CHIEFS is anticipating a response.

BAYO	(*Speaking solemnly*) I greet our fathers. Baba FAGBEMI said he will soon be here.
OLUPONA	Thank you, you may go.

(*BAYO leaves*)

I've never seen something like this in my life.
If we don't act fast, my people, much bigger danger is looming.

BOBAJOKO	In fact, we are acting late.
OLUPONA	Aigbo 'fa la n w'oke. Let FAGBEMI come, I know, definitely, Ifa will have something to say. If it is a sacrifice, Ifa will tell us.

FAGBEMI arrives

FAGBEMI	Mo ki eyin agba ilu.
ELDERS	We greet you. Aboru-boye bo-sise
FAGBEMI	Ase - - - e!
BOBAJOKO	FAGBEMI, thanks for answering our call. We are sure you know why we call you here. Yes. It's important that we know the cause of this calamity befalling us. We know, no oracle speaks without speaking of sacrifice; no divination as well will suffice without appeasement. Help us ask Ifa what the cause of this calamity is, and most importantly, to tell us what we shall do to appease the gods. *(Facing other CHIEFS). Abi, eyin oloye,* lest we are left in the dark.
ELDERS	It's true. *Ooto ni.*
FAGBEMI	It is true my fathers.

He sits on the floor, opens his quiver and brings out his Ifa articles and puts them in his left palm, covers it with the right palm and shakes it as he starts chanting Ifa eulogy.

Ifa olokun, the giver of joy
You're the custodian of knowledge
Orunmila, the Agbonniregun
All-knowing oracle
Tell us the truth, speak straight,
Speak not in riddles

He throws the articles on the floor

	(He is confuse) Eh!
ELDERS	*Ko ha si nkan o?*
FAGBEMI	*Ko si nkankan.* No problem.

He packs the articles, repeats the process.

If particle is blown off a child's eyes
The child sees clearly. ...

*He blows it and throws it on the floor again. He looks into it very well.
Then he starts speaking in riddles.*

Alara said they should enquire from
Ifa
What are the items of appeasement?
To avert evil
That the land may be peaceful in his
own time
Ifa, on the contrary said they should
dance

And celebrate, and make their way to
the forest
And crown Iroko, king over all trees
So shall there be peace
Like a river in the land.

A brief silence...

BOBAJOKO   FAGBEMI, what is the matter?
A word cannot be so hard to the
extent of slicing it with a knife.
Kini Ifa wi? Tell us?

FAGBEMI   *(Clears his throat)* Eyin oloye Alede-Ife
o,
I greet you once again.
Ifa said there is neither sacrifice nor
appeasement to avert this calamity.

ELDERS   *(With fear and surprise)* Ah! E - - - eh!
OLUPONA   Eh! Abomination!
Ifa kii bale ko ma wi t' ebo
Opele kii fohun ko ma wi t' etutu
Hawu! FAGBEMI, *hawu!*
A kii gbo laburu lenu Abore. Ki lo nje be?

FAGBEMI   Our ELDERS, Ifa said there is no
sacrifice.
But on the contrary,
Ifa said we should go to
Gbadegesin's family and make
ADEYEMI, ADEOLA's son our
king.

29

	And so shall peace reign in the village.
ADISA	We all know that our next king will come from Gbadegesin's family lineage, but we all know also that king making is not a thing of haste. We must do some sacrifices and then wait for some times. But before that time, are we not all going to die?
BOBAJOKO	What are we waiting for? After Ifa has spoken, must we wait as long as that? Don't we know why we normally wait that long? But now that the road is clear before our eyes, why should we waste time again?
FAGBEMI	Ifa said if we waste time; hmm!

FAGBEMI packs his things into his quiver and carries it. He's ready to go.

Awo lo! *(He leaves)*

As soon as FAGBEMI leaves, the two ELDERS (OJUMU and LADEPO) who are sent to Ilu-Moye now enter:

2 ELDERS	Eyin Oloye, a lo're, a bo're o
BOBAJOKO	Eja nbakan?
	What is the news?

Other ELDERS are attentive and eager

30

LADEPO	Oro 'un so sini l' enu, o bu 'yo si o, eyin oloye.
	It's a knotty issue.
	The priest over there said there is no sacrifice
	Except to go and make peace with Olofa-Ija village.
ADISA	Confusion! This is confusion! Baba Adifala in Ilu-Moye is a renowned Ifa Priest. He has never lied. We all know that. FAGBEMI is also a trustworthy young priest. Ifa himself appointed him as a second person to the late Ifa Priest. He will never lie. But how can two of them contradict themselves? I mean how can they say two different things?
BOBAJOKO	Did he say they are the one behind our disaster?
LADEPO	I asked him the same question but he said Ifa wasn't specific.
OLUPONA	It's even an abomination, or how can one make peace with his sworn enemy? It is never done anywhere. We shall not make peace, we shall fight them instead. Won't they say we are cowards if we attempt to make peace?

OJUMU	He even said if we don't act fast, I'm afraid; he said the next group of victims are the rest of us here.
ADISA	Isn't that better if death should take our lives instead of taking the lives of our leaders of tomorrow?
BOBAJOKO	Eewo! Abomination! Iku ye gere l' ori t' emi. Death has let pass of me. Emi ti p' eran okete. Iku ti re mi kete.

He taps his fingers over his head and leaves, other CHIEFS also dismiss.

Curtains close

Scene 3

The medical personnel are giving treatment to the people on the second day. One of them who is a preacher is speaking with Prince ADEROPO- the son of the late king.

ADEROPO	Our people from the city, we really thank you for your generosity. The gods of our land will reward you. I'm just coming from my fiancé, Awelewa's house. She is really

responding to the treatment given to her. She confessed it with her own mouth. In fact, before, she couldn't eat at all and if she managed to eat something, whatever she ate would either come out through her anus immediately or through her mouth. And within just five days, she has become as thin as a stick of broom at the same time pale and scrawny. However, before I left the place just now, in my presence, she has finished a mountain of amala with ewedu soup. *(He smiles)*. We thank you my brother.

DOCTOR   Let us give thanks to Jesus.

ADEROPO   You mean that Jesus personally attended to my fiancé. Where is he? Our people must have told him that Awelewa is my fiancé. I must personally show my gratitude to him.

DOCTOR   But you are not affected. Are you?

ADEROPO   No I'm not. The gods protected me.

DOCTOR   But the gods didn't protect other people, why?

ADEROPO   My brother, everything is destiny.

DOCTOR   But who are those gods. They must be caring.

ADEROPO   Ah! They are very caring and powerful.

Seven gods rule and protect this village. They are:

Alagemo- the god of ease,

Owiwi- the evil bird,

Orogodo-gbamiomio- the evil spirit of the jungle,

Aroni-gidigba- the god that lives in the valley of death,

Aganyin- the god of war,

Esuku- the god of the evil cafe and

Agidimo- the god of the dunghill.

You see, my brother, this Agidimo that I mention last eats *iyan onikoko*. That is yam that is badly pounded; *(he smiles in admiration)*

It is also our god of harvest.

DOCTOR	Wonderful! Thanks a lot my prince.
ADEROPO	You are welcome oga dokita. I want to leave now, tell Jesus that Prince ADEROPO will come to say hi to him tomorrow.
DOCTOR	No problem my prince. Please make sure you take care of your beautiful fiancé Awelewa.
ADEROPO	Iyen je dandan. It's important. Thank you.

Curtains close
Act 5
Scene 1

34

Olofa-Ija Village

The palace is unsettled; the ELDERS are troubled about their king that travelled about a week ago. They invited AWOSOLA; their Ifa Priest to enquire from Ifa to know if their king is safe.

OLUKOSI	AWOSOLA you are invited to this council's meeting to help us consult Ifa, if KABIYESI is safe where he is because we are confused.
ADIO	KABIYESI has never spent a night outside this palace before now. We are disturbed.
DOPEMU	We've also sent out ten soldiers to go in search of him four days ago, That is apart from the twenty ESCORTs that followed him. The soldiers only returned this morning to tell us that they didn't see the king and the ESCORTs.
OTUN	That is the very reason you have to help us to ask Ifa, if the King is safe.
AWOSOLA	KABIYESI has never travelled without informing me about it, But I didn't know that KABIYESI is not in this palace for the past a week. Eyin igbimo ilu, e koo kere o.

OTUN	AWOSOLA, is this the time to pass blame? Please, tell Ifa to tell us if the king is safe, abi.
AWOSOLA	I've heard you.

He sits on the floor, opens his big calabash painted white and brings out some cowries in his palm, covers it with second palm and shakes it very well and starts some chants-

> Ifa whose house is full of wealth
> A counsellor for all purposes
> Short man that sees beyond a thousand hills
> A lone dweller of the evil forest
> Sacred eyes that sees lovers in their secret places
> You are the tiny ear that hears human's imagination audibly
> To you we have come
> For the mystery of life and death dwells with you

He throws down the cowries. He is shock

> Eh! *Eemo re o!* Abomination!

He abandons his articles on the floor and wants to flee but Olukosi prevents and grabs him.

OLUKOSI	*Hawu!* What is the problem? Why are you running away?
ADIO	Take it easy with the old man please.
OTUN	We have to take things easy with him. He has never behaved strange this way before.
ADIO	You are right OTUN. There is no flame without fire.
OLUKOSI	Yet an old man shouldn't behave that way. If we all run out after him in like manner, our women and children will laugh at us, won't they? Then what are we going to say is pursuing us? *Agbalagba kii maa n sa lagbalagba. Hawu!*

AWOSOLA returns gently.

OTUN	Baba, *agba kii soro bi ewe ke!* Adults don't do things like kids. What is the matter? Tell us. *(Quietly)* Is our king dead? *(OLUKOSI is full of indignation, he says not a word).*
AWOSOLA	Our CHIEFS, forgive me. What I saw in the face of Ifa terrified me
OTUN	Whatever you might have seen baba, that behaviour is not good enough for an adult like you.

37

AWOSOLA	*(Shakes head)* Forgive me. I saw a great conflagration, a very big fire burning everywhere. It almost burns my face. I saw a very big river of blood.
DOPEMU	*(Nods, giving sign of understanding)* That should be the sign that the king of Alede-Ife Village is coming against us. *(To AWOSOLA)* Tell Ifa to tell us what the solution is, that we may not bath in the pool of blood, that this fire may not burn us.

AWOSOLA sits on the floor again, packs the cowries into his palms, whispers and throws them on the floor. He looks into it very well. He repeats the process and looks into it again then, he speaks-

Ifa says a man from Kuruki must be our next king.

(All the CHIEFS look at each other with confusion)

OLUKOSI	Next king! Did Ifa say our king is dead?
AWOSOLA	I wouldn't know
OLUKOSI	Help us ask again, is the king dead, If he's alive, where can we find him?

AWOSOLA packs his cowries, speaks to them again and throws them on the floor as usual

AWOSOLA	Ifa says we should act fast because danger is looming.
DOPEMU	aba AWOSOLA, thank you. You may go now.
	Please you will see the king's messenger if we need your attention again.
AWOSOLA	Thank you. *(He packs his things and leaves)*
DOPEMU	We need to act fast truly.
OTUN	To do what? Does anyone of us know a Kuruki man living with us in this Land?
ADIO	We shall find out.

Some GUARDS bring in two brutally wounded ESCORTs among those that follow KABIYESI on his journey-

ESCORT 1	*(Panting)* We were attacked on our way to Ayedogbon Land by a host of archers. We were shot at a distance. They never wanted to know who we were.
OLUKOSI	What of our king?
ESCORT 1	(Still panting) As we were making all effort to escape KABIYESI, he was shot also and he fell immediately.

OLUKOSI	*A fi yin j' oye awodi eo lee gb' adiye.* You are saddled with a responsibility and you fail.

He dips his hand into his pocket and brings out a charm and throws it at the two ESCORTs. Both of them drop dead immediately. Other CHIEFS are so angry at his callous behaviour

DOPEMU	OLUKOSI! You are complicating the issue. *Hawu!* We all heard the explanation of this young man. The situation was beyond their control. He said they were shot at a distance. They tried their best after all. See, I've been warning you, if you don't get rid of this arrogance, you will meet your waterloo very soon. You must pack the two of them to your house and eat them.

They dismiss

Curtains close

Act 6
Scene 1
Alede-Ife Village

Medical personnel from the city are still giving treatment, people are coming one after the other. ADEROPO is around again at the venue. He believes life must go on after the death of his father. The DOCTOR sees him as he's approaching; he stands and shakes hand with him.

DOCTOR	The prince, I'm happy to see you this afternoon. How is your fiancé Awelewa?
ADEROPO	Oga dokita, well-done. Awelewa said I should greet you very well. She said would be visiting you. And hope you saw the messengers from the palace?
DOCTOR	Yes we did. In fact, we must confess that you've been very kind to us. We enjoyed the dried meat but we couldn't drink the water they brought.
ADEROPO	*(With care and surprise)* Why? The water is good. That is what we all drink in this land.
DOCTOR	*(Shakes head)* No wonder!
ADEROPO	*Omi gidi ni. Omi awon ebora.*
DOCTOR	The water is bad. It stinks because it is not flowing. And besides when one of your people took us there for investigation, we saw a lot of disgusting things inside like- dead

41

	lizard, dead toad, dead rat, rags and a lot of dried leaves. All these make the water poisonous. It is dangerous to your health and that is the cause of the calamity in this village.
ADEROPO	Do you think so? Our fathers drank this same water and lived long. How would the water now kill us- their descendants?
DOCTOR	The test we conducted for your people shows they all have cholera. This is as a result of this dirty water certainly my prince.
ADEROPO	No! *Ko gbodo je bee*. It can't be so. Our fathers drank this water in their own days and they lived long. Now that their spirits guide us, how would they not purify it for us, their children? Tell me. And besides, apart from rain water which we also drink in this village, for the past twenty five years that I've come to this world, I've not tasted any other water. So why am I not affected? Tell me.
DOCTOR	Well, well, let us leave that aside, my prince. Don't you dig well in this village? That could have been a very good alternative for you.
ADEROPO	We don't dig well here, it is our taboo. Even if we try it, we will not

	get water inside no matter how deep we dig.
DOCTOR	Has anyone tried it?
ADEROPO	I don't think so
DOCTOR	Why?
ADEROPO	It is a taboo to try it.
DOCTOR	A small girl took us to a stream close to us here. We tasted the water and it tasted good, but your people say you don't drink it. Why?
ADEROPO	We can't drink that one. It is an abomination. And besides, can good water ever come from the midst of conspirators?
DOCTOR	How do you mean?
ADEROPO	Oga dokita, oro po mbe. It's a very long story.
DOCTOR	Can you please tell me the story? You can brief it, my prince.
ADEROPO	It is very long but like you said, I will brief it. You see, oga dokita, my great grandfather king Oyewumi found this land of Alede-Ife a very long time ago. He was the first king of this village. After him, there have been seven kings. My late father KABIYESI Oba Adeyeye, the Alade-Ife of Alede-Ife Land was the seventh king after him.

DOCTOR	So, would you be the next KABIYESI of this village, my prince?
ADEROPO	No! Another person will be.
DOCTOR	Why?
ADEROPO	I am not destined to be. You see, oga dokita, I've loved to live a quiet life and I'm pleased with it that way. After my father's burial rite, I plan to marry Awelewa and then travel to a distant land.
DOCTOR	Why?
ADEROPO	I don't know, but I like to live like every other people. I want to live like those who are not from a royal family. I just want to be myself
DOCTOR	I like your sense of simplicity.
ADEROPO	Thank you my brother. So like I was saying, my late father was the seventh king of this village. My father said his grandfather said, the first king of Olofa-Ija village was a bosom friend of king Oyewumi.
DOCTOR	The two kings were friends! That was a very good foundation. That means the two villages must be friendly.
ADEROPO	On the contrary, we are sworn enemies. Though they have been very good friends in the past until a certain time.
DOCTOR	When? What happened?

44

ADEROPO	I will tell you my brother. The first king of Olofa-Ija village gave his first daughter Princes Adunola in marriage to the first son of his friend, king Oyewumi. The first son of king Oyewumi was Prince Ademola. After the first and second king of Olofa-Ija village joined their ancestors, king Bedunje was their third king and that was when the problem set in. King Bedunje was a proud and wicked king. By the time Bedunje was their king in Olofa-Ija village, the second king, Oba Ademola was still on the throne in Alede-Ife village here. It was not long when Oba Ademola too joined his ancestors. Oba Adedara became the third king of our village here. When Oba Adedara became the king of our village, Oba Bedunje was still on the throne in Olofa-Ija village and like I said earlier, that was when the problem started to manifest.
DOCTOR	How?
ADEROPO	Oba Adedara had a son. That son was his only child. His name was Oyelami. The king loved and satisfied this son with everything. Not only the king was proud of Prince

45

	Oyelami, the whole villagers were also proud of his humility and his composure.
DOCTOR	That is good. Jesus too wants us to be humble.
ADEROPO	Jesus too likes that?
DOCTOR	Yes He does.
ADEROPO	You will show me Jesus before I leave so that I will deliver Awelewa's message to him.
	Like I was saying, our ELDERS taught us to be humble and obedient in this village and we obey them, except a very few bastards among us that choose to be wayward.
DOCTOR	Jesus is obedient to His father too.
ADEROPO	Jesus must be kind.
DOCTOR	Yes He is. My prince, can you please continue the story now because your audience are already in suspense.

ADEROPO looks back and he sees some village youths, adult, men and women who have never heard the story before standing behind him, enjoying the story. He stops and tells them to find something to sit on and make themselves comfortable. When he sees that they are all sitting comfortably he continues -

So my people, there used to be a beautiful young woman coming from Alamoye village every five market days to trade in our market. My father said her name was Abike. Oyelami

46

saw and admired this young woman and he later proposed to her. It was not a journey of a day anyway. It took him a very long time before he could summon courage to propose to her. To make the whole story brief, this young woman agreed to marry Prince Oyelami and their love was serious. Their parents were happy about their love affairs too. So they appointed a wedding day but something went wrong.

A male voice from the midst of the crowd

A MALE VOICE	What went wrong, my prince?
ADEROPO	Abike went missing. All effort to find her proved abortive. The two parents were disturbed.
DOCTOR	That would be too painful for the king's son.
ADEROPO	Too painful. By the time they saw Abike, it was Elewuro, the son of the wicked and proud king Bedunje, the third king of Olofa-Ija village that stole her. He has been envious of her love with Prince Oyelami. His father, king Bedunje gave him a charm called *mayehun* and a magic ring called *oruka amudo* to enchant the poor girl and unfortunately, he was successful. He satisfied all his immoral desires on the poor girl and by the time Abike would come back to her senses, she thought it was too late to go back to

her true love- Prince Oyelami. She thought he would not forgive her therefore, she sent a message of apology through her friend to the prince and the prince was very happy that at last Abike has been found. He sent her friend back to her affirming he still loved her but unfortunately, before her friend got back to her over there, Abike has committed suicide.

A voice from the midst of the audience

VOICE Kai, kai, kai. Ah! Too painful! She shouldn't have killed herself.

DOCTOR Jesus can forgive the worst sinner. I'm enjoying your story, my prince.

ADEROPO Thank you my brother. It was painful to the prince though, he didn't fight so as not to destroy the love between the two villages. But after a long time, the two kings died almost at the same time, and their two sons reigned after them, Oyelami became the forth king of Alede-Ife village here while Elewuro became the forth king of Olofa-Ija village as well. Elewuro was as proud and wicked as

48

	his father. He finally broke the friendship bond of the two villages.
DOCTOR	How?
ADEROPO	He sent a remembrance message to king Oyelami. After a while, he sent some GUARDS to go and seize King Oyelami's wife and bring her to his palace.

Another voice from the audience.

VOICE	Se o n sinwin ni? Is he insane?

ASAKE, OLUBUNMI's mother, who has also been listening, asks in anticipation-

ASAKE	So what happened, my prince? Were they successful?
ADEROPO	No. They failed. King Oyelami was a powerful but sensible and gentle king. But after they failed, their army came against our village but just fifty of our soldiers destroyed them and the wicked king himself. King Oyelami wouldn't have fought back but his army were so confident, they crossed the boundary and entered our village. Eyin naa ee rii pe aseju ti wo o? So these two villages, according to my father, had been

very friendly until the reign of king Bedunje of Olofa-Ija village and his son Elewuro who finally ruined the amity.

A male voice from the audience.

VOICE   A king that gave his people good time
Forever remembered shall he be
And a king who spoilt good time for his people
Will he not be forgotten as well,
For breaking the chain of love
Tied with pains and sweat.

DOCTOR   So what about the stream?

ADEROPO   Thank you. Since that time, my father said this village has done away with all that has to do with Olofa-Ija village. And since the source of that stream is situated at Olofa-Ija village, our fathers from that time said no son or daughter of this village shall fetch the water again. So we prefer to drink our own water of agony than to drink the milk of comfort that comes from the midst of a people who betrayed their friends.

DOCTOR   Was there any spell placed on the stream or on whoever uses the water?

50

ADEROPO	I don't think so my brother. If there is, KABIYESI would have told me.
DOCTOR	Is that why you've not been using the water?
ADEROPO	We just have to obey our fathers.
DOCTOR	Would VILLAGERS be drinking it now that they know that the water is not cursed?
ADEROPO	We shall not drink the water that flows from the midst of betrayers. We shall not drink the water belonging to our enemies.
DOCTOR	*(Brings out his Holy Bible)* Psalm 24 says; The earth is the Lord's and all its fullness The world and those who dwell therein. . .
ADEROPO	Who said it?
DOCTOR	*(Raising his Holy Bible)* This is the word of God. So God is the owner of the water not the people of Olofa-Ija village. Start to use it as from today.
ADEROPO	Which of the gods? Is it Owiwi the evil bird or Agidimo, the god of the dunghill or which one?
DOCTOR	None of them. I'm talking of God of all gods.
ADEROPO	You mean Eledua, the head of gods

DOCTOR	Do you know His son Jesus Christ?
ADEROPO	You promised to show him to me before I leave.
DOCTOR	Yes. He was the one who rescued Awelewa your beautiful fiancé from death. He died so that she may not die. He died so that you and all these people may not die. Jesus Christ is so caring. He used His own blood for the sacrifice to avert the calamity befalling this village. He loves you all. If you can just tell Him you love Him too and give your life to Him, then he will save your life.
ADEROPO	Show him to us, let us appreciate him.
DOCTOR	He is here in our midst.

Everybody looks around to see if they will see the Jesus

	You can't see Him with ordinary eyes. You need spiritual eyes to see Him.
CROWD	Spiritual eyes!

The little OLUBUNMI, *who has recently joined the crowd, speaks.*

OLUBUNMI	I saw Jesus yesterday night
ADEROPO	(*Surprised*) You! Where did you see him? Do you have spiritual eyes?

52

DOCTOR is interesting; he looks at the little girl with a surprise

OLUBUNMI	I saw Jesus when I slept.
ADEROPO	What did Jesus tell you? Did he tell you anything?
OLUBUNMI	Yes. He said His name is Jesus and Prince of Peace.
	He said all the gods are not true God.
CROWD	E - - - eh!
ASAKE	You! You are lying. Don't mind her, prince, she's my daughter.
ADEROPO	You mean— Agidimo, Aganyin, Owiwi, Esuku, Alagemo, Orogodo-gbamio-mio and Aronigidigba are not true God?
	(To the DOCTOR) Oga Dokita, don't mind the little girl. She's just kidding.
DOCTOR	Woman, it doesn't matter whether she's your daughter or not. She said the truth. All other gods are fakes. They can't save you. See, only Jesus can save you in this village. If you accept Jesus Christ today, if you die, you will live again.

ADEROPO thought within himself at this point that it must be true. After all where are the seven gods when KABIYESI and people of the village are dying like chickens whereas Jesus rescued Awelewa and the remaining people?

	My prince, your gods couldn't save the king and other good people of this village. If you don't accept Jesus now, this calamity will continue.
ADEROPO	If I die, I will live again! DOCTOR I want to accept Jesus, what do I do?

Some people, including OLUBUNMI and ASAKE, also join ADEROPO as DOCTOR prays for them.

ADEROPO	Have we accepted Jesus now?
DOCTOR	Yes, don't worship the fake gods again.
ADEROPO	What are we going to do to them?
DOCTOR	You can burn them with fire or throw them into the river.

A man's voice from the crowd

A VOICE	Ah! *Awon oosa ile wa!* The gods of our land! *Eewo!*

He leaves with anger. Then another woman speaks also.

WOMAN'S VOICE	Ibinu Aganyin o ma see ko loju! Nobody dares it. No one can withstand Aganyin's wrath.

DOCTOR   Those things are not God. My people, where is Aganyin when the king and your people are dying? But Jesus can save the dying people. He made Lazarus; a man who has died for four days lived again but none of your gods can even save itself or save you from this calamity. But Jesus has started.....

LADEPO   O to o nibi o baa de un! It's enough. You are turning the heart of our children against us. You told them to go and drink forbidden water and throw our gods into the river.

OLUPONA   What an abomination! Isn't these gods that our forefathers served and it was well with them .. that the land was productive and they were able to feed their numerous children? Were these gods not answering our prayers and protecting us?

E wo, e wo, e wa o, call your people together and leave our land. Leave us alone, leave our children alone and go

DOCTOR   Sir, what I am saying is the truth. .

OLUPONA   (Cuts in) I say leave us alone! Ai sa banii sun, ka fani ntan ya. Abi. We don't want to fight with you because of the fire burning the land at the present. Call your people together and leave. We give you three hours then if you refuse to leave, you may see another side of us. *(The CHIEFS leave with anger)*

Curtains close

Act 7
Scene 1

Olofa-Ija Village

The king makers are ready to install ADEOYE, the first son of their late king as the new king. This is contrary to the demand of Ifa since they cannot find any stranger from Kuruki to occupy the throne. They assemble at a shrine decorated with cloths of different colours. Some articles are placed in strategic places. The walls are painted in white and red with some scary images all around. The centre of the shrine is a sacred altar where they offer prayers to their gods. As soon as the Chief Priest finishes offering sacrifice, he calls ADEOYE to come and make his own request to the gods

ADEOYE   My fathers, what do I say?

CHIEF PRIEST	Make your request known to the gods. Your wishes for the land, for yourself, for anything. But be careful that you don't by mistake utter a negative word. Whatever you say can never be reversed. Our land that is barren is as a result of the mistake Elewuro, the forth king of this village made. He cursed the land in the process of making request. So be careful.
ADEOYE	Thank you the Chief Priest. *(He clears his throat)*

Ogbo leaf says you should hear me
Ogba commands you to accept my words
If ekolo speaks, the earth opens
The word that *okete* speaks to the earth
The same the earth obeys
Let our spirit mothers, that lives in the second world
Hear my words this day
Let the invisible powers that rule the secret places of our land
Accept my request
If *Opa Ebiti* falls, it falls forward
Let me always go forward in good things

	With left and right *eyele* brings good things
	Let good things be ours in this land during my own time
	Let goodness never cease in our land
	Fate was kind to Alara
	The land was peaceful in Alara's time
	Let our land be peaceful in my own time
	Fate was kind to Ajero
	Ajero became the spirits' favourite
	Let the spirits that have the power to break and build
	Make me their favourite
	As I ascend the throne of my fathers.
KING MAKERS	Aseeeee!

As soon as the king makers responded to his prayers, ADEOYE falls and dies.

	Eh! Abomination!
ADIO	I said it. I said it. I've said before that what we want to do is dangerous. My people, how can we go against the order of Ifa and go scot free? Tell me. I will leave this village for you.

ADIO leaves, king makers are baffled. They stand and look aghast. No one speaks a word.

Act 7
Scene 2

The same day in Olofa-Ija Village

This devilish afternoon, the day is terribly brightening. The noise of weeping from every side overwhelms the atmosphere. Each of the CHIEFS has lost either his wife or a child. The BEREAVED in the village too bring their dead ones to the frontage of the king's palace but in the palace is also a greater tragedy. The CHIEFS are around to speak to them.

BEREAVED 1   (*Crying*) I've never seen an evil as great as this in my life.

BEREAVED 2   Ah! This is terrible. See how my two sons macheted themselves in the farm. Let the king come out and do something. My children must come back to life, if not, I will kill myself right here in your presence.

OTUN   Our people, please be patient. As you can see, we too are not folding our arms. We are all casualties in this matter and nobody will say what is happening is not painful. May Orofo, the god of peace help us put an end to this evil.

BEREAVED 3 (*Rolling on the floor*) Let KABIYESI himself comes out. Let him come and witness what is happening to us oooo!

OTUN We understand how you are feeling. KABIYESI himself has travelled in search of solution to the problem and we know that peace will soon reign in the land.

BEREAVED 3 Are you telling me that you can't do anything to restore my dead child to life? I'm a widow. This is my only child, eyin oloye e dakun e saanu mi, don't let my child die just like this, plea - - - se.

ADIO Our people, like OTUN has said earlier, as you are looking at all of us here, every one of us has lost either a child or wife. Even now, Prince ADEOYE is dead too. That is why we are here. . .

BEREAVES (*Cuts in*) A - - - ah! Eemo re e oooo!

BEREAVED 4 Eh! What is happening? If the fire is burning, even in the palace, where shall we run to? Ah! This is evil!

ADIO By now we don't need to hide anything from you again. Uh! The king himself has joined his ancestors.

The **BEREAVED**	A-ah! Eemo ree ooo!
CHIEFS	*Hawu - - - u*! Baba oloye, a whole you!
	How can you say such a thing?

A mentally disadvantaged man passes by and speaks to them

MAD MAN	A great woe has betided our land
	That a human head can never fathom
	An explanation of what our spirit mothers' desired
	A living king is on a journey
	A king on a journey has joined his ancestors
	That our king is dead, isn't it good news
	That my two fingers are merged
	And a cat and a dog turn to a sheep
	And this gulf and rift of partition is bridged?
	I go; I go in the trail of love *(he goes away and everyone looks as he goes)*

Curtains close

Act 8
Scene 1

It is now a week that the Medical Personnel have left the village. More people, including LADEPO have died again, living the village more pathetic and confused. ADEOLA, an educated man of about fifty years of age, who is working in the city, arrives in the village with his son ADEYEMI today. The CHIEFS are there to welcome and discuss with them in ADEOLA's house.

BOBAJOKO   We thank our two CHIEFS that were sent to the city. You are welcome back to our midst. We greet our Prince and his son ADEYEMI too.

ELEMONA   Se oko o j' epo o

BOBAJOKO   ADEOLA, you and your son ADEYEMI must have been well informed about why we are all here this day. Like you must have been told, we are here because of your son ADEYEMI. Ifa has chosen him to be our next king and we must prepared him for that purpose immediately.

ADEOLA   Thank you our fathers. In fact, the two CHIEFS have already told us everything when they came to us in the city and we are very happy. Since ifa has chosen him, it is a thing of joy for us. The CHIEFS and I have

	spoken to him and he has agreed and was happy as well.
ADISA	Eledua o ni doju ti o.

The CHIEFS are very happy and cheerful. ADEOLA's wife, MOJISOLA enters and places a big cooler of wrap pounded yams and vegetable soup in their midst and departs to the kitchen.

BOBAJOKO	Thank you, our wife.
MOJISOLA	Thank you sir
BOBAJOKO	*(To the CHIEFS)* Let us hear from Prince ADEYEMI himself.

ADEYEMI who is sitting beside his father stands up.

ADEYEMI	*(Smiles)* I've not agreed! *(His countenance changes, the CHIEFS look at each other with surprise)*
	My fathers, I agreed and I didn't agree. I mean I'm confused. The same Ifa that appointed me here has also appointed me to be a king somewhere else. So tell me now if that can be possible.
CHIEFS	Abomination!
ADEYEMI	I think you can now see why I am confused, that it is an abomination and can't be possible.
OJOMU	*Eyin oloye e je ka se suuru na o.* Please let's be patient.

	(To ADEYEMI) How did you know that you have been appointed to be a king in another place?
ADEYEMI	My fathers, just last week Monday in Kuruki, the principal of my school sent to me that I was having some visitors. On getting there, I met two elderly men; they told me in the presence of our school principal that Ifa has chosen me to be their village king.
ADEOLA	*(Looks embarrassed)* What do you mean? You mean something as serious as this is happening and you chose to keep it to yourself. Did you tell us? You didn't tell me and your mother about what you just said? Please, our ELDERS don't mind him.
BOBAJOKO	*(Clears his throat)* See, my prince, this is your father's land, and we've been greatly troubled because of you. Because of you, the gods rejected our libations. You will be our king. Please forget about other people.
ADEYEMI	My fathers, I've heard you. These men also told me of their own predicament and it was so pathetic. So my fathers, I need to think about this matter.

64

OLUPONA	Time waits for no man and besides, who are these people? Which village are you talking about?
OJUMU	I doubt it if they are not ELDERS from the enemies' village
ADISA	No, it is impossible, they can't be the one.
OJUMU	It is possible. They've always liked to take whatever belongs to us
ADEYEMI	Who are the people you are talking about sir and what makes them our enemies?
OLUPONA	They are the people from Olofa-Ija village, a village close to us here.
ADEYEMI	But like my father would always say, we are peaceful people, can we not make peace with them?
OLUPONA	No! We are light and they are darkness.
ADEYEMI	Even so my fathers, light will illuminate darkness. Because the light shines into the darkness and the darkness cannot comprehend it.
OJOMU	We don't understand you.

BOBAJOKO gestures to other CHIEFS and they grab ADEYEMI and hold him with intention to carry him away for installation preparation but he escapes and flees.

ADISA	We must get him now!

| **BOBAJOKO** | Leave the young man alone. He is our king, Ifa has spoken. |

Curtains close

Act 8
Scene 2

ESAN, an energetic young man, fully kitted in Alede-Ife army's costume is running with all zeal towards his late father's power house. Some village ELDERS are wondering what is happening or why he is running. He enters the house and suddenly brings out the Sword of Vengeance. The ELDERS, who know what it means to bring out the sword, grab him but cannot, collect the sword from him.

ESAN	*(Full of energy and anger)* Ye - - es! The time has finally co - - me!
OJOMU	*(Forcing the sword out of his hand with a few incantations)*
	ESAN, give us this sword. What is wrong?
	Ero pese ni t' igbin
	Iran eja kii gbona lale odo
	T' ojo ba ro, ara a tu 'le, tu 'gi oko
	K' ara o tu o pese
	Give it to me!

ESAN   No - - - o! The time has fully come to show that the gentility of a lion is not for cowardice!

Women from the farm are running into the village. The village becomes disruptive. The army dress in their costumes, each with his weapon, prepare for war. Singing war song and beating war drum, people are running helter-skelter.

WOMAN 1   E gba wa oooo! Awon ara Abule Olofa-Ija ti k' ogun wo 'lu oooo!

By this time, the village ELDERS now understand why ESAN carries the sword.

OLUPONA   ESAN, give us this sword. You can fight them without this.

ESAN   The time has come. Let's use this sword just this once and let the story ends here.

OLUPONA   What do these people want from us this time again? They will never be tired of war. What's their problem?

ASAKE runs to them fearfully and delivers a message

ASAKE   *(Hurriedly)* Eyin oloye, Baba JAGUNLABI said he wants to speak with you and our young man here. *(She runs back as fast as she can).*

67

OJUMU	ESAN can you hear that? Baba said we should come with you.

As they walk along, the drums are still beating hard; the army are arranging themselves in strategic places. ESAN and the CHIEFS enter JAGUNLABI's house.

CHIEFS	*(Prostrating)* K' ara o le o baba
ESAN	*(Knees down, still breathing hard)* Baba o
JAGUNLABI	Eyin oloye ilu mo ki yin o.
	(To ESAN) Sheathe the sword and give it to me!
ESAN	*(Breathing hard)* Ah! Baba *(he sheathes the sword and releases it reluctantly)*.
JAGUNLABI	This sword can destroy the whole world.
	It is too powerful to be used
ESAN	These people have been disregarding what we can do for long, Baba,
	Is this how we will be silent forever?
	Now they are kidnapping our women,
	Are we still going to be silent?
	They carried out an arson attack on our farms of numerous crops.
	Father, for how long are we going to remain without using this sword?
JAGUNLABI	May be forever!
	We used it once;

But we will probably not use it anymore. (*A footstep is hard*)

Who is that in the passage?

A young man of Alede-Ife soldier walks in, breathing hard

	(*To the young man*) What did Olofa-Ija Village say they want from us this time?
YOUNG MAN	(*one of his knees on the floor*) They said we kidnapped their king to be, my father, They said we either surrender or they destroy us completely.
JAGUNLABI	OLUPONA, go and tell them that we have surrendered.
OLUPONA	Insult!
JAGUNLABI Go!	

OLUPONA leaves.

JAGUNLABI	OJUMU, go and look for the boy, you and other CHIEFS, and bring him here.

OJUMU departs

YOUNG MAN	My father, let us face them.

	We all know they cannot withstand us
JAGUNLABI	(*Smiles*) I was the former BALOGUN of this village. I know they can't withstand our army, But they like to make trouble. Don't let us follow their folly. If we do again, their innocent children will become fatherless; Their innocent women will become childless and widows.
ESAN	Since I've grown up to know a lot of havoc these people have caused in this village, You have never, for once, allowed us to fight back, why? They've made so many of our women, widows and some of our little ones, fatherless too. Why should we still not fight back?
JAGUNLABI	Because we are men of peace. You are a youth, and the blood of youth boils. We are never cowards, but we are men of peace. Let my foolishness guide you, my sons.
ESAN	My father; please, give us a chance to use this sword,

	They are fast approaching us.
YOUNG MAN	Baba, without this sword; can't you let us fight them back?
	They are fast approaching our boundary.
JAGUNLABI	They won't cross our boundary the third time.
	Their fathers should have told them history.
ESAN	Which history?
	We are told that you used this sword in your own time.
JAGUNLABI	You see, like I said, I was the former BALOGUN of this village. These troublesome people looked for ways to call us to war that time but they couldn't find one. Then they thought if they could hurt me, since I was the chief of the village soldiers, that I would surely be provoked. Therefore, they killed my wife Omoremi and my two children in the farm.
ESAN	Ah! These people are too wicked. Was that why you used the sword?
JAGUNLABI	No! We didn't use the sword. My son, this sword is too powerful. You can't understand. It can destroy the whole world.

ESAN	Ah! My father, you didn't use it! Would that suggest you didn't love your wife and two children?
JAGUNLABI	I love my family. My love for Omoremi didn't allow me to remarry till today. I know she will be waiting for me in the second world. I love her. I hope to see her one day.
ESAN	So, why did you use the sword?
JAGUNLABI	They crossed our boundary. They crossed our boundary, then they were approaching the palace, to kill our king. Even though we had power to prevent them that time, we could have resisted them alone and choose not to engage in fire fight with them, yet their confidence, sarcastic words and arrogance irritated me so much that I allowed my anger to misguide me.
ESAN	Misguide! Don't we all need to be angry in the face of provocation?
YOUNG MAN	We do of course!
ESAN	Then, how did you use it my father?
JAGUNLABI	So you don't even know how to use it already. I won't tell you. I know, this sad history ignites your curiosity, and so, I won't tell you again.

YOUNG MAN	Our father, please, we want to share from your wisdom. How did you use it? Please tell us Baba.
JAGUNLABI	(Smiles) You too are curious to know how I used it. I know. I know you are reading it and capturing the pictures in your mind. But more than just this sweet tale, I wish also you read and capture the fact therein and internalize them. Don't worry I will finish the story.
ESAN	Thank you my father.
JAGUNLABI	I pointed the sword at the mid-day sun The sword shone in anger The day became terribly brightened And there came a mighty wind Accompanied by a great fire Sweeping the host of their army and village
ESAN	Then what happened?

JAGUNLABI I shed tears. I was moved to tears

YOUNG MAN & ESAN   Why?

JAGUNLABI	Because in my attempt to fight evil, I justified the evil

YOUNG MAN & ESAN   How?

JAGUNLABI	In the death of their innocent wives and children

YOUNG MAN & ESAN   (*sighs*)

ESAN (*Lamenting with tears*)

Ah! AKINLABI o!
AKINLABI my brother!
Should you die as a fool dies?
Should you die as a man who has no
friend?
AKINLABI, a fiery fighter in the
battle field
A violent wind that terrifies the brave
and the weakling
O! You are caught in your ignorance
of the time and season
And died like a toothless tiger
I loved you!
But forgive me, forgive me
Please forgive my failure
To avenge your blood.

JAGUNLABI   Wipe your tears son. We have to let
the past be gone. These two villages
have been very friendly in the past.
Their love they shared without
rancour
Let us return to that first love
Let us burry this Sword of
Vengeance
And fight instead with the Sword of
Wisdom and the Sword of
Forgiveness
For the most painful thing you can
do to your enemies
Is to forgive them

74

The best way to win a battle
Is not to let it happen
Let us tell them they have won this
battle
E je ka pe were ni buoda
Ko baa le je ka raye se tiwa

The CHIEFS enter with Prince ADEYEMI

BOBAJOKO	My father, here we come.
JAGUNLABI	Yes, you will go with ADEYEMI now, hand him over to them, since he likes to be their king.
OJUMU	Baba; that is a hard thing to do! How can we hand over our son to the enemies? And besides, he's our king that we expect to bring peace to the land.

JAGUNLABI Go!

BOBAJOKO	We've heard you and we will do just as you said. We know your wisdom has helped this village many times in the past. But father, can their scorpion cease to be scorpion?
JAGUNLABI	Yes, their scorpion will cease to be scorpion if you remove its sting. *(To ADEYEMI)* My son, come to me. You are a son of this land. We have morals, we have values. Don't throw your morals to the dog. Your

75

great grandmother, Adunola, was a princess of the first king in the land of Olofa-Ija. That king gave princess Adunola to Ademola the second king of this village as a symbol of peace. Therefore, though they may not know, and may not know that you are from this village that they think we kidnap you yet, you should know that you are not a stranger in Olofa-Ija Village. (*Holds ADEYEMI's right lobe*)

Remember the son of whom you are! Don't disappoint us. The gods will guide you about what to do.

ADEYEMI My father, may God guide us.

JAGUNLABI You may now go, but make sure you don't fight with them.
For if you want peace,
You will accept pains.

They leave

Curtains closed

Act 9
Scene 1

Battle front

76

The drums are beating hard, there are gunshots everywhere. The noise of war from the two sides shakes the ground. One of the soldiers of Olofa-Ija village is chanting ofo at the top of his **TOWN CRIER** when the **CHIEFS** arrive at the scene with **ADEYEMI**.

OLOFA-IJA VILLAGE'S ARMY (*Evoking the gods of their land*)

> Ebora nla ti n gbenu afefe dagboru
> Orisa gbangbanran ti n gbe nu ojo mi odan
> Alujannun rogbodo, rogbodo
> Ti n gbe lagbede meji aye atorun-
> Oju kongba-kongba ti n p'omo lekun t'osan t'oru
> Eyin orisa metalelugba l'orita meta isalu orun
> Ebora nla ti n gbenu ogbun ainisale ile
> Aronigidigba ti n mi'gbo mi'ju laiberu
> I call upon you all this day, come and fight for us

The drums are still beating hard with gunshots everywhere. BOBAJOKO holds ADEYEMI and walks gently to the other side of the boundry, walks through the front of the soldier, looks at him and shakes his head as he's still evoking their gods. Their CHIEFS are also around with costume of charms on their body. BOBAJOKO walks towards them and hands ADEYEMI to them.

BOBAJOKO	*(Kneels down)* My fathers, here is your king. You are the winner, we fear your anger. We don't want to fight again. We are too stubborn and stupid. Our folly makes us behave foolishly like this and wanted to fight all the time. We know you are men of peace. Please forgive us and let this war end.

As this is happening, the CHIEFS of Alede-Ife village call their army to cease fire. DOPEMU, one of the CHIEFS of Olofa-Ija village speaks-

DOPEMU	*(Laughing loudly, he suddenly gives BOBAJOKO a blow in the mouth)* Foolish people, who taught you wisdom You would have let us destroy you completely We are the winner, you are the looser.

He turns to other CHIEFS and shouts aloud

	We won!
OTHER CHIEFS	Winner!
DOPEMU	Shall we forgive them? They call us father

OTUN   Let us forgive the cowards

(*All these sarcastic statements and the blow pain BOBAJOKO. He almost reacts but he remembers JAGUNLABI's words, so he bears the pain*)

DOPEMU   (*To BOBAJOKO*) Stupid man, stand up on your feet, we forgive you You may now go

BOBAJOKO   Thank you our fathers. (*He departs*)

Olofa-Ija village CHIEFS call their army together to stop the drums and the shooting and ask them to return home

DOPEMU   (*To ADEYEMI*) Our king, you are welcome.

ADEYEMI   I will be your king on one condition!

OTUN   On one condition! What condition our king?

ADEYEMI   Can these two villages become one?

All the CHIEFS are speechless, remembering the calamities befalling their village. They look at one another, nobody want to be the first person to speak

DOPEMU   (*Aside to OTUN*) What shall we say?

OTUN   (*Quietly*) What do you suggest? You know this will never happen. (*He gestures to other CHIEFS to come closer*) this is absurd, what shall we say?

79

EGBEMODE	You know we don't have time to debate, let's say yes, but we know what we are doing. Don't we?
ADEYEMI	*(Insisting)* My fathers, can Alede-Ife and Olofa-Ija villages become one?
EGBEMODE	*(Clears his throat)* Yes our king *(None of them says a word again)*
ADEYEMI	If so let's go
OTUN	My king, should we send to them immediately?
EGBEMODE	Don't let us do it that way. Let everything be settled and then we shall know how to go about it.
ADEYEMI	Eyin baba oloye let us go to village. Truly, to reconcile is not a problem.

On their way to village, ADEYEMI asks the CHIEFS

	My fathers, do you know Jesus?
CHEIFS	No, we don't know him
ADEYEMI	*(Smiles)* Jesus said "Do to people What you want them to do to you"
OTUN	Who is Jesus?
ADEYEMI	Jesus is the Prince of Peace and the King of kings
DOPEMU	King of which land?
ADEYEMI	I will tell you when we get to the palace

Curtains close

Act 10
Scene 1

Alede-Ife Village

CHIEFS from Olofa-Ija village come to make peace with the people of Alede-Ife village. They are sitting under a cashew tree at the centre of the village. Alede-Ife village **CHIEFS** sit at one side while the **CHIEFS** from the second village sit at the opposite, facing each others. In the centre of the meeting ground are some evocative items (*of Olive branch and the leaves of the Jade plant tied together, broken arrow and broken rifle tied together and cola nuts*) that Olofa-Ija village **ELDERS** bring. **OTUN** their **SPOKESPERSON** speaks.

OTUN   *(Clears throat)*
Our ELDERS, honourable and sagacious
Let not your tolerant heart
Loath our innocent presence
For to love we must now return
(Paused)

Wise are you, our fathers and

81

Like a beast devoid of understanding
Are we, your lowly servants
Forgiveness we seek
Forgiveness we plead
For in your humility, wisdom you
taught us
And in your tolerance you taught us
knowledge.

Folly has bewildered a simple man
He follows his father's errors
With this lucidity we come therefore,
To right our wrongs

Forgiveness is great
Forgiveness is power
Let forgiveness rule your heart
Like sunlight rules the day

Love is forgiving
Love is uniting
Let love smile in your heart
Like the night moon upon our roof
As we make our request of
amalgamation

*Alede-Ife village ELDERS stand up immediately with all joy, and
alacrity, shaking hands with and embracing them.*

ADISA	*(Raises hands)* Muso! Muso! Muso! Muso!
All CHIEFS	E - - - eh!
ADISA	Muso! Muso! Muso! Muso!
All CHIEFS	E - - - eh!
BOBAJOKO	You may all have your seat

They all sit down, except BOBAJOKO who is still standing

Our brothers, you are welcome
We don't have much to say
For you've said it all.

Hmm! The only way to move
forward in life
Is to agree and disagree
But if we disagree my people
Let's guide against resentment
For resentment is deadly as cholera is
It poisons our peace of mind
It makes one drink the water of
agony
So that we remain in the grief of
death

Therefore our brother, we've both
won this battle
In offer and acceptance.

Muso! Muso! Muso! Muso!

83

CHIEFS	E - - - eh!

They sit to drink. They bring together their chairs to form a circle. They share cola nuts among themselves and drink. As drinking is going on, ADEROPO enters and gives them message from JAGUNLABI.

ADEROPO	Greetings to my fathers. Baba JAGUNLABI said you should all see him when you finish the meeting.
BOBAJOKO	Thanks, we will surely do that. Tell him we will come
ADEROPO	I will deliver your message

ADEROPO turns to go, BOBAJOKO calls him back to have his own share in the cola nut and palm wine

BOBAJOKO	My prince, come back. Take this and celebrate with us *(he gives him palm wine and cola nut)*
ADEROPO	*(Collects it)* Thank you, my father

He quickly drinks it, returns the calabash and leaves

BOBAJOKO	Yes, you are welcome, my prince. *(Aside to OTUN, the SPOKESPERSON of the Olofa-Ija village CHIEFS)* That is the most sensible youth in this village. Everyone is proud of his humility and composure.

OTUN	Un-uh! That is very good of him. *(He drinks)*
BOBAJOKO	He's the prince of our late king. He's affable, intelligent and easy going. We are planning his marriage towards three market days to this time.
OTUN	That is very good, my chief, *(he drinks)*. Baba oloye, do you know Jesus?
BOBAJOKO	No.
OTUN	Jesus doesn't harbour resentment"
BOBAJOKO	Who is he?
OTUN	Jesus is the Prince of Peace and the King of kings
BOBAJOKO	King of kings? Where is he?
OTUN	Let our KABIYESI come; he would tell you more about Him
BOBAJOKO	Prince of Peace! King of kings!
OTUN	Yes. *(He finishes his drink)*

They all finish their drink and move at once to JAGUNLABI's house.

Curtains close

Act 10
Scene 2

The ELDERS of the two villages are in the boundary of the two villages. JAGUNLABI addresses them and gives them the Sword of Vengeance so that they will bury it.

JAGUNLABI   I've long created this day in my mind, and it's a thing of joy that we all witness it today. You see my people; as long as this sword remains with us, we shall know no peace, therefore, please help me to remove these palm fronds *(pointing to the palm fronds)*

The CHIEFS remove the palm-fronds to reveal a waiting grave

Thank you, I prepared this grave for myself when I thought I would die before now. But since the death has refuse to come for me, take the Sword of Vengeance and burry it inside. Meanwhile, before you do that, take this digger and dig it one feet more.

He gives them the sword and the digger, BOBAJOKO collects them. They dig the grave so that it measures 7 feet. BOBAJOKO drops the sword inside the grave. They shout for joy.

BOBAJOKO	Muso! Muso! Muso! Muso!
CHIEFS	*(With joy)* E - - - eh!
BOBAJOKO	Muso! Muso! Muso! Muso!
CHIEFS	*(With joy)* E - - - eh!
BOBAJOKO	Eruku fun euku
	Erupe fun erupe

They throw dust on the buried sword. JAGUNLABI comes first, BOBAJOKO follows, the new king arrives the scene, and follows BOBAJOKO before the rest of the CHIEFS do their own in turn until they completely cover the grave with sand.

BOBAJOKO	I think we should adopt a new name for this great kingdom since we are no more two.
JAGUNLABI	Since the idea comes first to you, you will be the right person to suggest a name before other people.
BOBAJOKO	*(Smiles)* O dara bee baba. It's good *(pauses and looks up)* I suggest, IFESOWAPO.

Everybody yells and claps in acceptance

JAGUNLABI	We are not through for now. Let everybody find somewhere to sit. *(Pointing to the wall that separates the two villages)* This *Wall of Separation* must be pulled down. It has significantly

hindered our friendly interaction and expansion. This *Afara of Access* destroyed long ago must be built again. So, let two ELDERS go to Alede-Ife Quarters and two ELDERS should also go to Olofa-Ija Quarters to bring our youths to perfect the work. The palace of our new king shall be built in this place.

Curtains close

EPILOGUE

After some hours, the ELDERS return with the youths and within some hours, the youths demolish the wall and those constructing the *afara* do a very good job.

After few weeks there is a tremendous change in IFESOWAPO Kingdom. People are now fetching Omi-Ayiye Stream. The Government Agency for Health Service comes back to Alede-Ife Quarters. There is announcement in the radio that the request which the new king of Ifesowapo Kingdom, KABIYESI Oba ADEYEMI, Onife of Ifesowapo Kingdom made concerning the establishment of Primary Health Centre and Primary School and Potable Water has been approved.

Mmap Fiction Series

If you have enjoyed **Sword of Vengeance** consider these other fine books in **Mmap Fiction and Drama Series** from *Mwanaka Media and Publishing:*

The Water Cycle by Andrew Nyongesa
A Conversation..., A Contact by Tendai Rinos Mwanaka
A Dark Energy by Tendai Rinos Mwanaka
Keys in the River: New and Collected Stories by Tendai Rinos Mwanaka
How The Twins Grew Up/Makurire Akaita Mapatya by Milutin Djurickovic and Tendai Rinos Mwanaka
White Man Walking byJohn Eppel
The Big Noise and Other Noises by Christopher Kudyahakudadirwe
Tiny Human Protection Agency by Megan Landman
Ashes by Ken Weene and Umar O. Abdul
Notes From A Modern Chimurenga: Collected Struggle Stories by Tendai Rinos Mwanaka
Another Chance by Chinweike Ofodile
Pano Chalo/Frawn of the Great by Stephen Mpashi, translated by Austin Kaluba
Kumafulatsi by Wonder Guchu
The Policeman Also Dies and Other Plays by Solomon A. Awuzie
Fragmented Lives by Imali J Abala

https://facebook.com/MwanakaMediaAndPublishing/

9 781779 243225